REVENGE OF THE ESSEX GIRLS

Cathy Hopkins & Alison Everitt

Robson Books

First published in Great Britain in 1992 by Robson Books Ltd, Bolsover House, 5-6 Clipstone Street, London W1P 7EB

British Library Cataloguing in Publication Data
A catalogue record for this book is available from the British Library

Typeset by Spectrum Typesetting Ltd, London
Printed in Great Britain by Butler & Tanner Ltd, Frome and London

CONTENTS

She who can lick, can also bite (old Essex saying...well, OK, it's an old French proverb, but it was probably inspired by a visit to Essex)

THE AUTHORS

Cathy Hopkins and Alison Everitt are a great disappointment to their parents whose comment on seeing their latest offering was 'they should know better at their age and ought to get "proper" jobs.'

After seriously considering this sensible advice, both girls felt they had to stay true to their vocation and chose to continue to write 'mucky' books. Their other books include: Cathy's: *Girlchasing: How to Improve your Game, Manhunting: A Girl's Guide to the Game, 69 Things To Do When You're Not Doing It: The In-Between Lover's Handbook, Keeping it Up: How to Make Your Love Affair Last Forever,* and *The Joy of Aromatherapy* (not a mucky book!). Alison's are: *The Condom Book For Girls, That's Fashion* and *The Modern Girl's Book of Torture: A Realistic Look at Health and Beauty.*

photograph by Martin Riedl

THE RESEARCHERS

With thanks to our research girls without whom the book would not have been possible.

INTRODUCTION

Have you ever wondered who started the Essex girl jokes? I can tell you. It was Brian, a telephone salesman. And what a prime example of pretty average manhood he was, with his saggy Y-fronts and lily-white bum.

Anyway, he picked up my mate Ginnette one night, got her in the back of his second-hand Vauxhall Cavalier and tried the business. Now Ginnette, like most true Essex girls, has done the rounds and, not wanting to suffer further indignation in the local clinic, legs akimbo as a team of spotty first-year medics poked and prodded: 'Dilated to see you, ha, ha, ha! So that's where I left my pen! ha, ha, ha, now, open wide miss...'

'No condoms. No sex,' declared Ginnette as Brian was finishing off his rather predictable foreplay (inspired by an old episode of the 'Golden Shot' – left a bit, right a bit, er, left a bit...again, ready to fire...)

Now Brian hadn't come prepared, and so, he didn't come at all. That is, until later when he went back to his hotel for the late-night adult extra channel film *Headless Bimbos Can't Say No*.

But what would he tell his mates the next morning? They'd want details, souvenirs and scores out of ten. Now the average British male when confronted with failure usually either blames someone else or makes a joke of it. Brian chose the latter and the Essex girl joke was born. Again.

And so all the gags that had circulated about Jewish

princesses in the seventies and 'dumb blondes' in the fifties found their way on to fax machines all over the country. 'Hoh, ho, yo, ho,' roared all the other salesmen nation-wide, many having had a very similar experience with Ginnette when they were in Essex and thankful that at last they could laugh off the shame of being caught WITHOUT their trousers down!

NB: This was also the start of the term 'a right Brian', a rather apt turn of phrase used to describe the typical dork we poor girls have to contend with, and believe me, he's not only found in Essex.

A FEW TYPICAL

RIGHT BRIANS

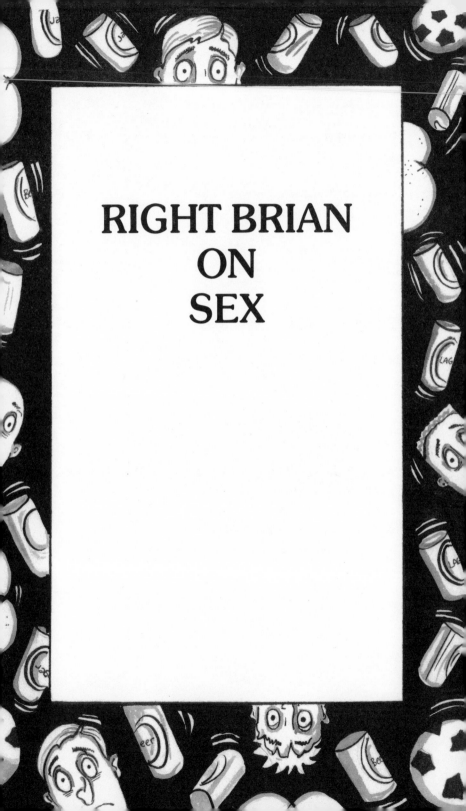

RIGHT BRIAN
ON
SEX

What's the similarity between a right Brian and old age?

They both come too soon.

What's the difference between a pub and a G-spot?

A right Brian can usually find a pub.

What's the similarity between a right Brian and a bottle of cheap sherry?

They're both lousy liquors.

What's the similarity between a cheap firework display and a right Brian?

One mediocre bang and the evening's over.

Why doesn't a right Brian believe in an imminent Messiah?

To him, a second coming is beyond the bounds of probability.

What's the similarity between a right Brian and a football player?

They both dribble when they're trying to score.

RIGHT BRIAN
AND SEDUCTION

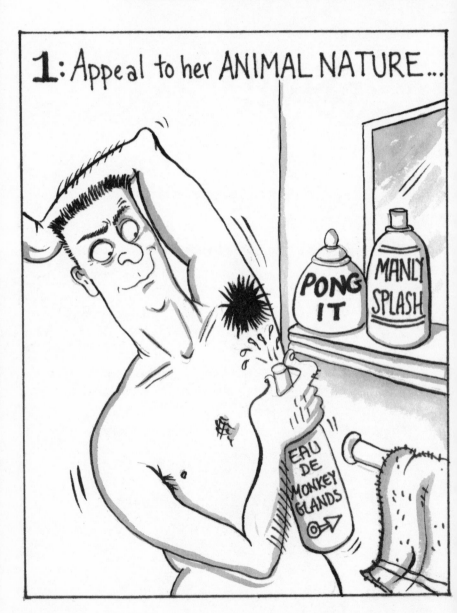

TECHNIQUES...

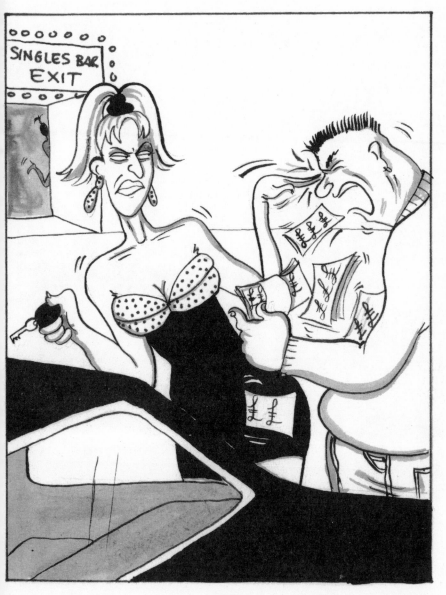

17

What's the similarity between a modern injection and sex with a right Brian?

It's all over before you feel a thing.

What's the similarity between a right Brian's bazooka and a rocket?

Once it's gone off, it disappears into oblivion.

What's the similarity between sex with a right Brian and a straw hat?

Neither is felt.

What's the similarity between sex with a right Brian and a Hepatitis B injection?

A quick, short prick in the backside and it's finished.

What's the similarity between a right Brian's privates and an ice-lolly?

They both disappear into nothing when you suck them.

What's the DIFFERENCE between a right Brian's privates and an ice-lolly?

An ice-lolly doesn't mind if you bite a bit off and chew on it.

What's a right Brian's idea of foreplay?

You awake??

What's the difference between sex with a right
Brian and an Opal Fruit?

*Right Brians can't come in four refreshing fruit
flavours.*

What's the similarity between a right Brian and a deadly cobra?

No one in their right mind'd get into bed with either of them.

How many right Brians does it take to screw in a light bulb?

Impossible to find out because no one'll own up to screwing WITH a right Brian.

How do you know when a right Brian's had an orgasm?

Snoring.

What's a right Brian's only chance of ever coming into money?

A girlfriend with gold caps on her teeth.

THINGS THEY SAY...

...TO GET YOU TO HAVE SEX

What does a right Brian say when told that during sex 100 per cent of men have an orgasm compared to only 4 per cent of women?

Who cares?

What's a right Brian's favourite hymn?

Oh come, oh come Emmanuelle.

RIGHT BRIAN
ON
RELATIONSHIPS

DOUBLESPEAK

IS WHAT HE SAYS WHAT HE'S THINKING?????

What's a right Brian's idea of a serious commitment?

OK, I'll stay the night.

What's the similarity between a right Brian and a mortgage?

The interest is unwelcome and the demands never end.

What's a right Brian's idea of the perfect woman?

3 foot-high, large mouth and a flat head to rest yer beer on.

But right Brians also have their uses!!

'My Oberon, what visions have I seen. Methinks I
was enamoured by an ass.'

More uses for a right Brian...

...When there's nowhere to park...

...As a letter rack...

...When you need somewhere to store the cold drinks...

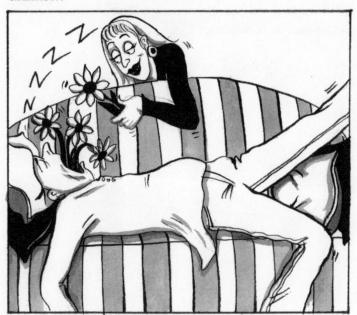

...As pure decoration...

What's the similarity between a right Brian and a flight balloon?

Both are full of hot air.

What's the only time a woman'll succeed in changing a right Brian?

When he's a baby.

What's the similarity between a right Brian and a stamp?

One lick and they stick to you.

What's the similarity between a right Brian and a dog?

One stroke and they follow you everywhere.

Where will you find a faithful right Brian?

Solitary confinement.

44

WHAT TO DO WITH AN UNFAITHFUL RIGHT BRIAN!

INSTEAD OF BLAMING HIM, TRY A

NEW APPROACH, GET TO THE

ROOT OF THE PROBLEM;

PERHAPS HE'S BEEN UNDER

TERRIBLE STRESS AND STRAIN

AT WORK THAT FORCED HIM TO

ACT IN AN UNCHARACTERISTIC

WAY, SO WHY NOT TRY A LITTLE

ALTERNATIVE THERAPY,

STARTING WITH ACUPUNCTURE.

AT THE CLINIC

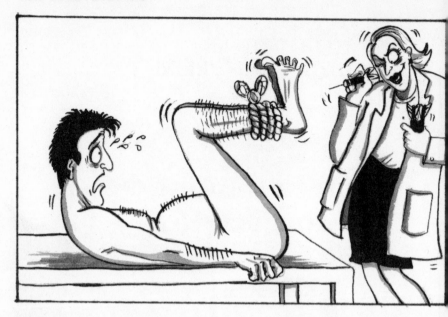

OR FROM THE COMFORT OF YOUR HOME, GIVE HIM THE ACUPUNCTURE DIY TREATMENT

AND IF HE DOESN'T RESPOND TO THAT THEN YOU MAY HAVE TO RESORT TO METHODS HE WILL UNDERSTAND!!

WHERE TO FIND

...At the weekend...

...At Christmas...

A RIGHT BRIAN

...At childbirth...

...At the prospect of NOOKIE...

Why do right Brians like wearing green suede?

Because it matches their teeth.

What happened to the right Brian who cleaned his ears out?

His head caved in.

What's the similarity between a right Brian and the state of the British economy?

Both are in terrible shape.

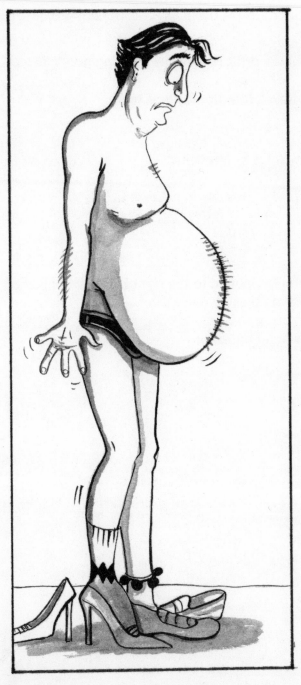

What's a right Brian's favourite thought of the day?

Look up a friend.

Why does a right Brian eat beans every day?

Because he loves to take daily bubble baths but can't afford a jacuzzi.

What's the similarity between a right Brian and a riding stable?

Both are either vacant or full of shit.

When invited for cocktails, what did the right Brian get when he asked for 'a slow, comfortable screw up against the wall'?

A tangy highball.

What happened to the right Brian who put odour-eaters in his shoes?

He disappeared.

What's the similarity between a right Brian and greasy hair?

Both tend to be lank, limp and lifeless when you want a bit of body.

What's a right Brian's favourite film?

Gone with the Wind.

Why do right Brians like being legless?

It's their only opportunity to boast that their plonkers touch the floor.

What did the right Brian do to expose himself to culture?

Went flashing in the local art gallery.

RIGHT BRIANS THROUGH HISTORY

What's the similarity between Adam in the Garden of Eden and a right Brian?

Both came first; men always do.

What's the similarity between a right Brian and Herod?

Neither knows what is required when asked to give head.

But it was in fact Julius Caesar who was the first to sum up the persona of a right Brian when he spotted a bunch of them waiting to do battle with him after his first invasion.

According to one ancient Essex girl,
Julius turned out to be a disappointment
and a bit of a right Brian himself.

Hamlet was another early right Brian, judging by his obvious confusion over how to please a woman:

'To bed, to sleep, perchance to dream of better ways to come. Aye, but where do you rub?'

What's the similarity between a right Brian and Guy Fawkes?

Both have a limp fuse when it comes to a blow job.

And right Brians seem to have followed
in their forefathers' footsteps ever since.

What's the correct technical term for when a right Brian's girlfriend has an orgasm?

A miracle.

What's the similarity between a right Brian and a bus?

Neither comes when you want them to, then just as your patience has run out, they come all at once.

What's the difference between a right Brian and a cucumber?

A cucumber stays hard for longer.

What's the similarity between a cake made with ordinary flour in the oven and a right Brian's privates?

They both get very hot but still can't rise.

What's the similarity between a right Brian's privates and a man with a broken leg?

Both have difficulty standing up.

What's the similarity between a right Brian's privates and concrete?

Concrete eventually goes hard.

What's the difference between a right Brian and an egg?

In 7 minutes an egg can be hard, in 7 minutes a right Brian will be soft.

What's the difference between a right Brian and a chocolate Treet?

Chocolate Treets don't melt in your hand.

It's been said that when it comes to right Brians there's not a lot there, in which case...

What's a right Brian's theme song?

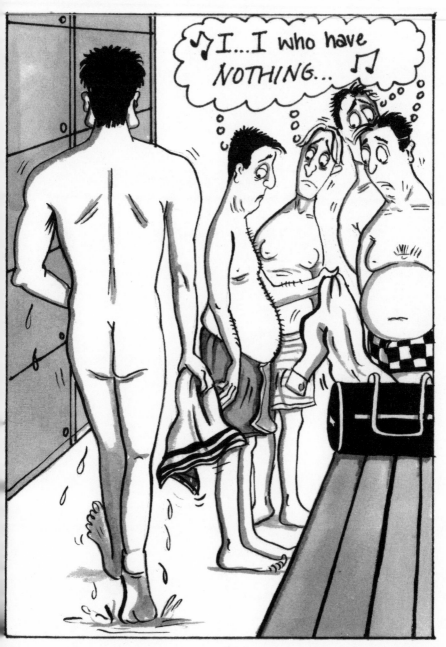

What's the similarity between a cheap butcher and a right Brian?

Neither has any meat worth displaying.

What's the similarity between a right Brian and a pair of ill-fitting curtains?

Neither is well-hung.

What's the similarity between a right Brian and a game of rugby?

Odd-shaped balls.

What's the similarity between a right Brian and car keys?

Both are easily mislaid.

What's the similarity between a right Brian and an old car?

They both need a lot of touching up before they can perform.

What's the similarity between a right Brian and a bad cello player?

They both sit and scratch their instrument instead of learning how to use it properly.

Why was a right Brian refused entry to the local golf club?

Because he couldn't match up to the stiff membership requirements.

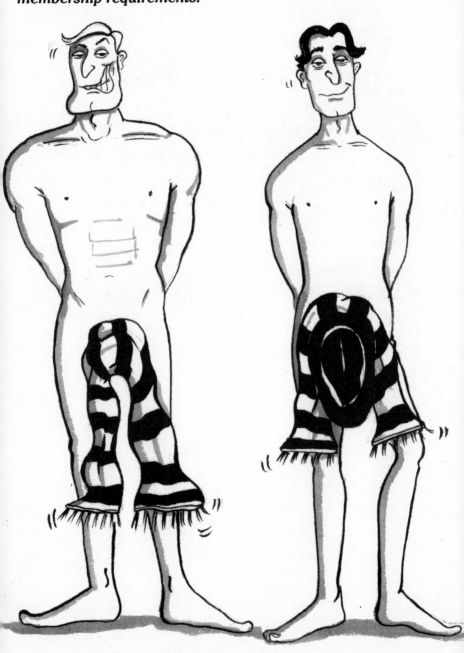

And sometimes,
the fact
there's not
a lot there
simply means
he's just
plain stupid.

What's the similarity between the brain of a right Brian and the English prison system?

Not enough cells per man.

What's a right Brian's favourite advertising slogan?

Go to work on an egg.

What's a right Brian's definition of boxer shorts?

Fallout.

What won't a right Brian stand for?

A woman on a bus.

What does a right Brian do on his fiancée's hen night?

Gets his pecker out.

What's the similarity between the local council complaints office and a right Brian?

Both are impossible to get through to when you need to talk.

At a tennis match, what does a Jewish right Brian say when the umpire shouts 'new balls'?

'So? Eva Goldstein's got a new nose but she's not telling everyone.'

What's the similarity between a right Brian and a baby?

A loud noise at one end and no sense of responsibility at the other.

Why can a right Brian never think straight?

Because he's always got curves on his mind.

What four-letter words offend a right Brian?

Don't and stop.

What's the difference between a right Brian's brain and a right hand?

More fingers on the hand than brain cells in the brain.

Why do right Brians only get half an hour for lunch?

So their bosses don't have to retrain them.

Having heard girls like men with a sense of humour, what does a right Brian do to make her laugh?

Shows her his privates.

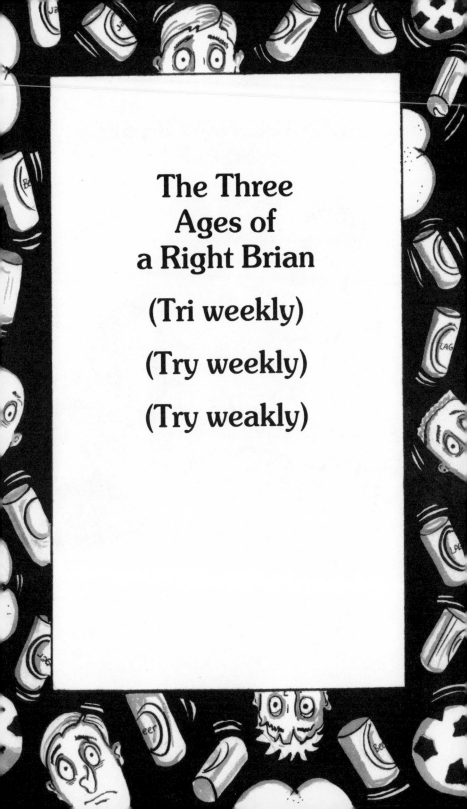

The Three Ages of a Right Brian

(Tri weekly)

(Try weekly)

(Try weakly)

TEENAGE: HOW HE SEES HIMSELF...

THE REALITY...

ADULT: HOW HE SEES HIMSELF...

THE REALITY...

OLD AGE: HOW HE SEES HIMSELF...

THE REALITY...

What's the similarity between a right Brian and an old record?

They both scratch a lot.

Why do right Brians hang about in bookshops?

They are looking for novel lovers.

What's the similarity between a right Brian and herpes?

Can't get rid of either once you got 'em.

What excuse do right Brians give for never taking their wives out?

It's wrong to go out with married women.

What's a right Brian's favourite song?

'Ain't too proud to beg.'

What does a right Brian say to a girl who's just told him that her body is her temple?

That he'd like to attend more services.

What's a right Brian's favourite food?

Crumpet.

What is the standard excuse that a right Brian uses for a rash on the privates?

Lipstick.

Why does a right Brian think there's a reference to sodomy in the Bible?

Because he read, 'Get thee behind me, Satan.'

What's a right Brian's opinion of cunnilingus.

He thinks it's one helluva tongue-twister.

What does a right Brian think of fellatio?

He thinks he's a character in Hamlet.

What's a right Brian's attitude to anal sex?

It's hitting rock bottom.

What happens to a right Brian when he hears someone talking about aural sex?

Pricks up his ears.

What's a right Brian's attitude to bisexuality?

If you can afford it, why not?

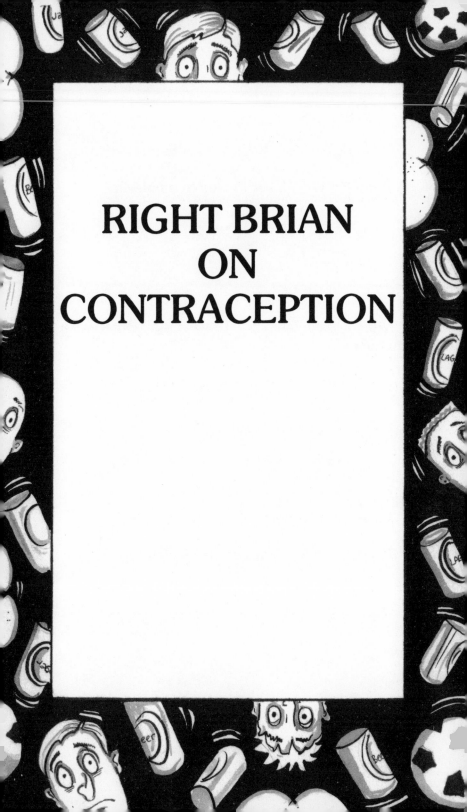

RIGHT BRIAN
ON
CONTRACEPTION

What does a right Brian think a French letter is?

What the French use to play Scrabble with.

What's the difference between a right Brian and a condom?

Condoms are no longer thick and insensitive.

When ought a right Brian to use contraception?

Every conceivable occasion possible.

What's a right Brian's attitude to circumcision?

It's a rip-off.

What does a right Brian think oral contraception is?

Talking your way out.

What's a right Brian's attitude to contraception?

If the cap fits, wear it.

What did the right Brian ask for when he needed a condom in Russia?

Little Red Riding Hood.

Why does a right Brian favour vasectomies?

Because he believes a stitch in time saves nine.

MORE ON CONDOMS (OR CONDOMS ON MORONS)

THINGS THEY SAY...

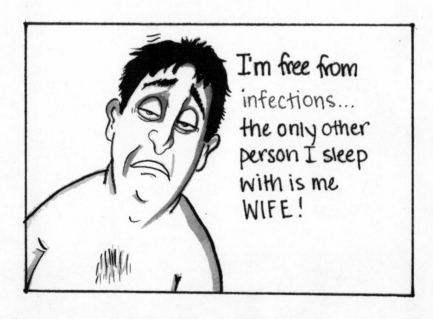

...TO GET OUT OF USING A CONDOM

What's a right Brian's idea of safe sex?

Masturbation.

What do you call a right Brian who uses the withdrawal method of contraception?

Daddy.

What's a right Brian's concept of fair play in a relationship?

Once with a condom, once without.

What's the similarity between a right Brian and a packet of condoms?

They both come in three sizes, small, medium and liar.

What is a right Brian's opinion of Johnny Cash?

He thinks it's change from the condom machine.

What's a right Brian's idea of DIY?

Rolling a cling-film condom.

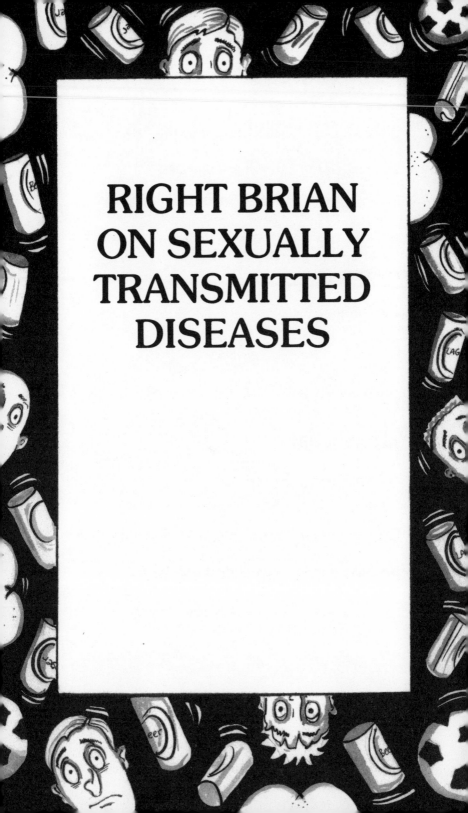

RIGHT BRIAN ON SEXUALLY TRANSMITTED DISEASES

What's a right Brian's attitude to the AIDS crisis?

The last one to catch it is a wanker.

What do you give the right Brian who has everything?

Penicillin.

What did the right Brian say when asked to name a Chinese venereal disease?

Ping-pong balls.

Why don't right Brians suffer from haemorrhoids?

Because they're such perfect arseholes.

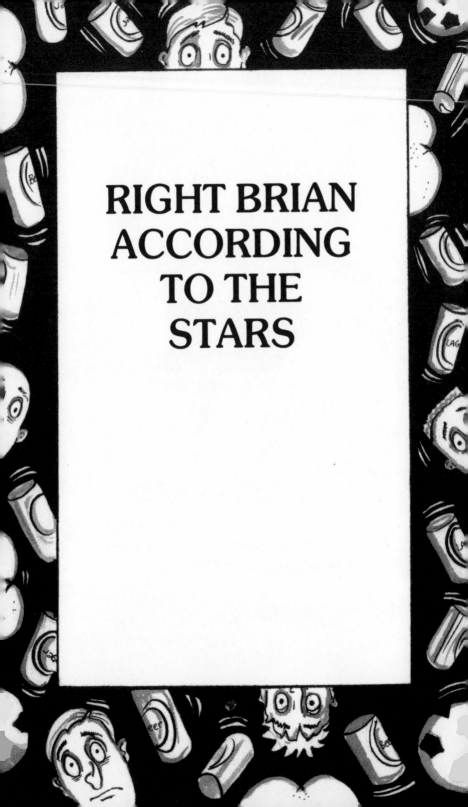

RIGHT BRIAN ACCORDING TO THE STARS

ARIES: Sign of the ram, never looks before he leaps and so usually leaps too soon! In other words – trigger-happy.

The Ram looks SHEEPISH.

TAURUS: Although thick-necked, prone to funny turns if he sees red and stubborn as a bull, the Taurean right Brian is happy as long as he's fed.

GEMINI: Sign of the twins, meaning he's either schizophrenic or two-faced and leading a double life.

CANCER: Sign of the crab; he walks like one too, especially when he's pissed.

LEO: Sign of the lion, a show-off who spends all his spare time down the hairdresser's.

VIRGO: A real prissy-knickers who folds all his clothes up before he gets into bed. Would have liked to have been a health inspector.

LIBRA: Libran men are usually members of the playboy club. Sadly right Brian couldn't come up with the membership requirements.

SCORPIO: The Scorpio right Brian has good reason to be secretive. He likes to dress up in leather and be called names...like Betty.

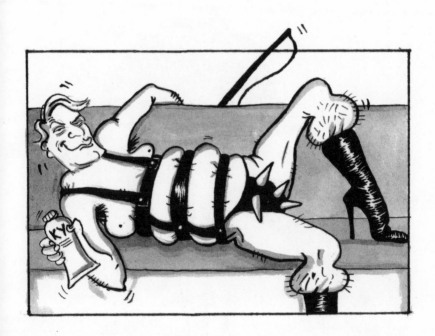

SAGITTARIUS: Half man, half horse, sadly, right Brians tend to get the halves in the wrong places.

CAPRICORN: The Capricorn right Brian is true to his sign – reliable, a hard worker and very, very boring.

AQUARIUS: The Aquarian right Brian sometimes seems to be on another planet altogether; either that or there's no one in upstairs. Einstein's theory $e=mc^2$ means energy equals matter. This can be applied to everything and everyone except the Aquarian right Brian who is nothing but a lifeless blob. Still, no matter.